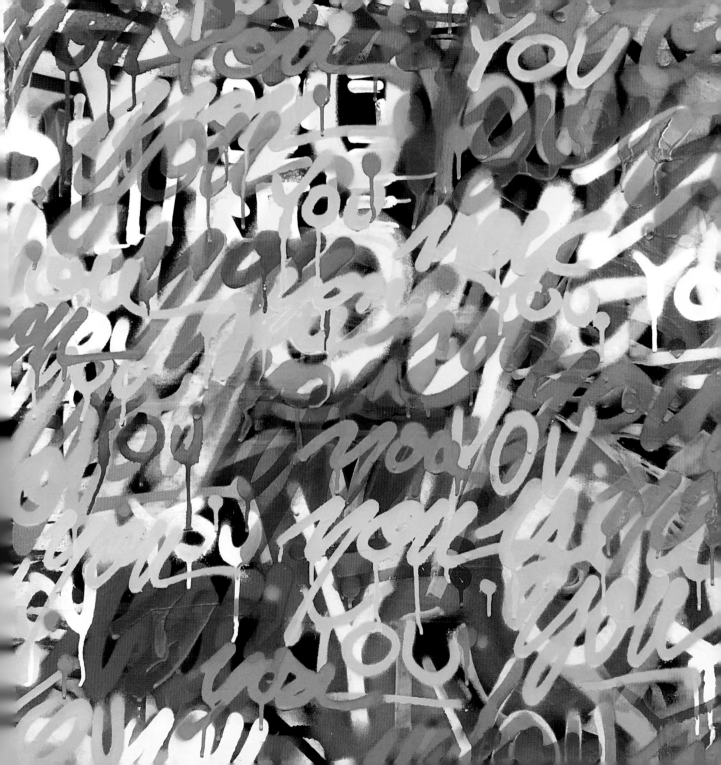

# DEDICATION

I would like to dedicate this book to my two baby girls, Ariana and Isabel, who daily remind me how beautiful life is; to my husband, Marcelo, who stood by my side through this journey in "giving a voice" to homelessness; and to my family and friends, without whom I'd be lost.

A special thank you to Jason Naylor, who created the cover art for this book; to Susan Rockefeller for being a huge supporter in bringing this book to life; and to the Help USA organization for partnering with me on this mission. Last, but not least, I would like to send a huge thank you to all the influencers, donators, brands, and communities that stood by me from the very beginning.

www.mascotbooks.com

## IT CAN BE YOU: HUMANIZING HOMELESSNESS

**For more information, please contact:**
Mascot Books
620 Herndon Parkway #320
Herndon, VA 20170
info@mascotbooks.com

Library of Congress Control Number: 2020918234

CPSIA Code: PRQ0321A
ISBN-13: 978-1-64543-432-0

Printed in India

# YOU

## IT CAN BE

## HUMANIZING HOMELESSNESS

JORDANA GUIMARAES

# Jordana
# *Guimaraes*

# AUTHOR, FOUNDER OF THE NYLON PROJECT

Being an entrepreneur comes with its own challenges, as money is slow to come by and fast to check out of accounts. Over a phone call, I recall that in early 2017 after the second Fashinnovation event, that I started to really feel the pinch and started to fall behind on payments, a pattern any new entrepreneur would be familiar with. I didn't realize how much money was going out and the fact that we were still a new company, so people didn't believe in us just yet.

Falling behind on two months' rent and not being able to afford insurance, my husband and I had a chat as we were close to missing the third month's rent and on the brink of eviction. We decided to go back to Brazil and stay with his mother until we could get back on our feet again. We left New York behind, including all of our beloved belongings such as kids' toys, furniture, and clothes; we only took the survival essentials to get to Brazil. Because of family, we overcame the struggle.

@ACLBYJOJO

Jason
Naylor

PHOTO CREDIT: DREW REYNOLDS

## COVER ARTIST

Jason Naylor is an award-winning artist/designer based in New York City, known for his bright colors and even brighter messages. Jason's work has received global recognition, including the Golden Novum Design award and two CLIO Fashion & Beauty Bronze medals. Jason has been featured on HGTV and the Discovery Channel. In 2018, Jason was named by Bumble as one of the 100 Most Inspiring New Yorkers, and his colorful creations have found partnership with brands like Coach, Guess, Pepsi, and Maybelline. Jason's mission is to spread color and positivity across the globe. His brightly colored designs and positive words reflect his zeal for life, his quest for joy and his love of LOVE.

Beatriz
*Adrianna*

**THERE WAS A TIME I HAD HIT A HURDLE.** I was balancing performing (music, dance, acting), attending auditions, a marketing position at a startup company, finishing my last semester to get my BA degree in business, and working on my blog that I had just started. I felt very overwhelmed and wasn't succeeding in any of the things I was pursuing. This was going on for several months before I made a big decision: focus my complete attention and give one hundred percent of myself to just one thing, in order to truly grow and succeed. After taking a holiday trip to clear my thoughts and figure things out, I made the big decision to quit my job, put school on hold, stop performing, and focus solely on pursuing my business blog, *Live Love Wear It*. I realized this was what resonated with me the most, felt most like myself, and made me feel the happiest. I took all of my savings, got the support from my favorite people, and went all in! Luckily, I didn't need to use much of my savings because I made sure to hustle hard in my new business endeavor. I do still have a love for acting, which I hope to someday continue pursuing. For now, I love what I do. I am happy to have made this decision, which has taken me to where I'm at today!"

## HOMELESS INDIVIDUAL

"I was brought up in a home where both of my parents never allowed me to be creative. I felt as though everything I wanted to do was forbidden. Therefore, when I turned sixteen, I started trying to do everything my parents never allowed me to do: singing, acting, modeling, and art. However, doing this without my parents' support and having never taken lessons kept me from succeeding. Because I did the opposite of what my parents wanted me to do, which was to get a college education and become a businessman, this resulted in them disowning me and putting me to work on the streets. Since I had no support from my family, I was on my own. It's hard to be on the streets as a kid trying to make something out of yourself in the arts. I never left the streets as it became my home. To this day, I entertain those who want to listen or watch. I don't know anything else, as this is the life I have chosen. . . all to be able to do what makes me happy."

@BEATRIZADRIANNA

# Braylen
# *Brooks*

# FORMERLY HOMELESS

"I think what makes my story so unique is that I've been denied so many times because I put my faith in the hands of others. I've been in Los Angeles for six years, and I've been denied by every single modeling agency or creative agency I've been to. I took matters into my own hands and said to myself: 'You know what? If no one is going to give me the opportunity, I'll give myself the opportunity.' I think my main purpose in what I do is to inspire, empower, and encourage people who share similar interests and have been through trials and tribulations. People never knew that I was homeless. I've never shared it with anyone. I've never allowed anyone to get close enough to me to where they would be able to figure it out. I just recently posted my testimony on Facebook because I felt like people were looking at my updates and thinking, 'Oh, he's spoiled. He's got to be. Must be loaded, and his parents are probably rich.' On the internet, it's so easy to paint facades. I wanted to share my true story so that people could understand that I am working and pioneering my way through this industry that I created for myself. More than anything, I really want to inspire and encourage others, which is much more important to me than simply showcasing myself on a luxury platform."

@BRAYLENBROOKS

# Camille
# *Newbern*

**" A FEW YEARS AGO, I LOST SOMEONE VERY CLOSE TO MY HEART.** Even though I think of him daily, it is around this time of year that his absence is most poignant. Nearly six years have passed, a lifetime in some respects, yet the memories remain as vivid as if they had happened mere moments ago. I try not to reflect with too much detail because the truth is: IT STILL HURTS. You never know which word or embrace will be your last. . .you just hope that you end with a good one because in the end, all we have are our memories. I am blessed that mine are rose-colored and lovely. Some people are in our lives for years and then leave without the slightest impression. Others pass through only briefly and change us at our very core. Soul mates, maybe? Not necessarily in a romantic sense, but more so that you were fated to meet for a reason, maybe because they were needed in your life at that particular moment.

I believe that sometimes, when their job is done, they move on whether or not you were ready to let go. They say that time heals all wounds, and I suppose that is true. However, a loss is a deep puncture to the heart. The pain is never as acute as it was in the beginning. The sharpness dulls to an ache. Eventually, the wound heals; however, it never mends to its original form. There's always a scar, and maybe it's no longer as painful, but it's always there—as a remembrance (I happen to like that), almost as if it's a tattoo on your heart as a reminder that you carry with you always. As much as I try to make some sort of sense of the whole thing, at the end, it doesn't really matter why or how. What does matter is that he was in my heart. He still is, and that is enough."

# HOMELESS INDIVIDUAL

"We met when we were eighteen years old. She was my first love, and I was hers. Throughout the many years spent together, we never had kids, mostly due to difficulties on my part. We decided to live a life where it'd be her and me forever. I always imagined us as Romeo and Juliet—not being able to live without each other, which remains to be a true statement. After being together for thirty-seven years, my wife fell very ill with cancer, and due to us earning minimum wage, the costs became too grandiose for us to keep up with the medical bills. I did everything within my power to save her; however, it wasn't enough. My wife passed away, and I was left with nothing. I lost everything, which, to me, was fine since I had lost my reason for living. I am now on the streets and hope to one day see her again. her smile is what keeps me going and warm from day to day."

Carlos
Romero

and I was born in Barcelona. I grew up in a humble family and district (Hospitalet de Llobregat, Barcelona, Spain). I spent all of my childhood between school and the streets, where I played soccer. My parents and sister were the ones who pushed me to follow my dreams despite all of the obstacles I found in my way. For this reason, I empathize with The NYLON Project. I believe in giving a second chance to everyone. I mean, everyone deserves the opportunity to have a dignified life. I work hard every day, looking for a way to leave my mark in this world by doing small deeds. Three years ago, I realized my passion is fashion and acting. Since then, I have focused all of my energy on that. Something I learned from my parents when I was growing up without much was: 'Don't cry to give up. Cry to keep going.'"

## HOMELESS INDIVIDUAL

"I grew up in the hood. Most of my family and friends had gone to jail at times for doing what they had to do so we could have food on the table. Those are my role models. There was and still is no way out for me. Since I wasn't born with everything handed to me, I did and still do what I know best, which is to do whatever it takes to make my day today. There is no time to think of whether what I am doing is good or bad. I just have to do what it takes to live."

@C.ROMERO.S

# Carolina
## *Lindo*

**" I BELIEVE THAT ONE OF THE HARDEST MOMENTS IN MY LIFE IS HAPPENING RIGHT NOW:** the moment when you realize that you are on your own and you have to face the reality of life. When you have to start from zero and realize that life is hard and not everything will be handed to you. You have to work very hard to achieve your goals and dreams. The only person that can help you is yourself, because if you don't do it, no one else will do it for you. Some people have it harder than others, but I believe that anything is possible. If you trust and believe in yourself, as well as being kind to others, you can achieve anything you set your mind to."

# HOMELESS INDIVIDUAL

"My every day is a struggle. I don't know my name. I was born into homelessness. I am not even sure what my age is. How do I go somewhere to work or have an opportunity to get myself out if I don't know who I am? I have the will but I'm not sure how to use it. Who will help me? It's tough, but I will keep trying. I just need some guidance. The problem is that those who want to help are not sure about what to do. I have always been on my own, therefore, I don't trust the system. Maybe one day."

# Christine
# *Kong*

**I DON'T THINK THERE WAS ONE SINGULAR EVENT THAT HAPPENED IN MY LIFE THAT I OVERCAME TO BECOME WHO I AM.** Instead, there have been a series of events, all of which have shaped me into a more confident, strong, and determined individual. I grew up in middle-class suburbia, where my immigrant parents owned small shops to provide for my two sisters and me. We didn't have excess, but we managed and tried to live like we blended in. I put myself through college, working and studying hard, vowing to live a more comfortable life than my parents did, and not wanting to bear any financial burden on my future children, which is the immigrant way of life. Don't get me wrong, my parents did the best they could, and in looking back, I wouldn't have had it any other way. Through their struggles, disappointments, and defeats, a fire arose within me to DO better, BE better, and LIVE better. It was not just one event that changed me. It was all the events along the way, such as walking home from school with a key around my neck to an empty home, to helplessly watching my mother go through breast cancer when I was ten. And then there were the times I begged my father to stop as he threw away our savings at the poker tables, and the embarrassment of downsizing our five-bedroom home to a two-bedroom condo when my parents lost their store. I remember the excitement I felt when I opened my acceptance letter from UCLA, my elation when receiving my first real paycheck from my first job out of college, experiencing love at first sight when meeting the man who would become my husband, and the incomprehensible joy and miracle of having kids. We are all fighters when we need to be. Each experience we live helps us realize our potential and urges us to decide to fight harder. We all have our moments. They can break us, or they can shape us. Rise above, and let it shape you."

# HOMELESS INDIVIDUAL

"Have you ever heard of the saying, 'when it rains, it pours?' Well, my entire life has felt like a never-ending downpour of rain, without any popping out of the sun. There were times that I looked up and asked whoever up there is in charge, 'How much more can I take?' We as humans can only take so much, and after a while, it starts to drain you, and you lose hope. I didn't have anyone there to help me dry up from all those downpours. Without any love and support, it's hard to snap out of the anger and defeat. At least, living on the streets, I understand that things will always be bad rather than thinking everything will be okay, especially when you find out that your parents are addicts or that your brother has been abused (and there is nothing you can do). That when you're hungry, there is no food to be found and there is no light at the end of the tunnel. Here on the streets, when someone gives me a little love by feeding me or giving me some money to buy my favorite chocolate, it's a great day, and I don't expect anything less or more."

@DAILYKONGFIDENCE

Claudia
Salinas

**I WAS A VICTIM OF BULLYING, ESPECIALLY DURING JUNIOR HIGH SCHOOL.** I was the nerdy, stick-thin-framed girl, which made me an easy target. Whenever I was better at something than the others, I was bullied. I got slurs all of the time because I danced ballet and was into music and art. I was an outcast in a lot of ways. In high school, there was this girl who constantly tormented me. She used to steal my clothes, burn my car seat with a cigarette, and scratch my car with her keys on a number of occasions. She was bigger than me, and whenever she was around, my heart would start to pound. I felt like I was going to vomit because she physically pushed me around and verbally abused me. I remember one time when she punched me, and my face landed in a tub full of peanuts.

I didn't fight back. I just stood my ground and stared at her. I allowed myself to be bullied because I was scared and didn't know how to defend myself. All of those dark moments made me extremely insecure at the time, but I also developed a thick skin with strong ambition. I used all of these experiences as fuel for my future. It's kind of crazy, but everything that you get picked on for or makes you weird essentially is what's going to make you excel and sexy as an adult."

# HOMELESS INDIVIDUAL

"Have you ever felt different than others? Felt as if something about you just wasn't quite right? I was born with the inability to speak without slurring. I was never able to pronounce certain words, like the other kids. My single mother got tired of trying to teach me and felt that she had failed when, in reality, it's just not possible for me to speak like everyone else. I got made fun of, but so did my mom, which made it worse for her because the ridicule came from her neighbors and friends. My mother started drinking to run away from her problems. In turn, I wound up feeling ignored and neglected. I left home, and in the hopes of finding solace on the streets, I found that I was more accepted and finally didn't have to live a life of shame. To this day, I hope my mother has found happiness."

@MISSSALINAS

# Derek
# Warburton

# FORMERLY HOMELESS

"I have seen great darkness, but now I live in the light. Gratefulness is the only word I can use to describe my childhood and survival. Being homeless, mentally abused, bullied, and wanting to end my own existence has given me the strength to fight for myself and for the good of others. I live my life to the fullest. I will never forget where I came from, and at the end of the day, all that matters is kindness and love. I have been blessed to be the international Goodwill Ambassador for clean water for Just a Drop and the Style Ambassador for the city of Los Angeles for the ten years I've worked with the homeless. I have a philosophy: today may be tough, but tomorrow can be the best day of your life. Live it!"

@DEREKWARBURTON

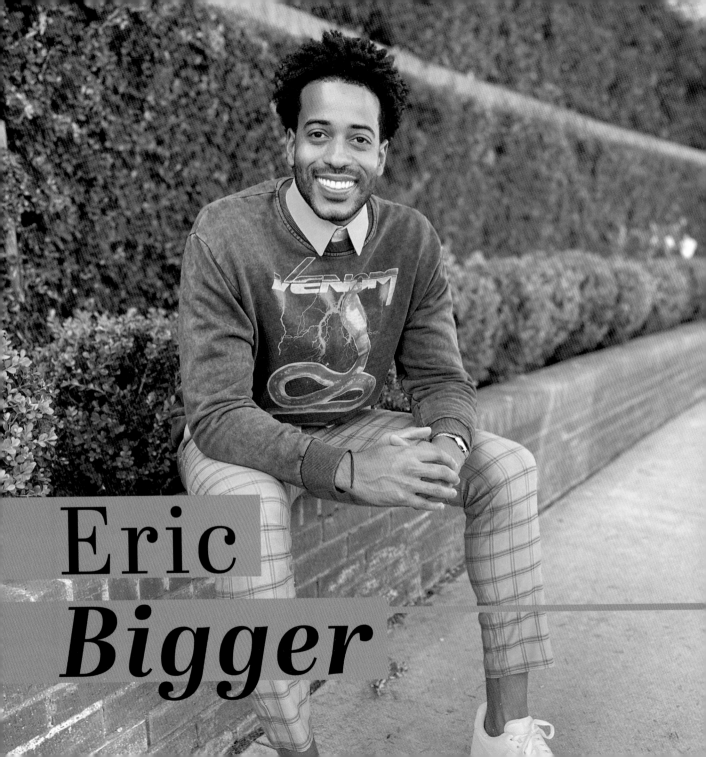

Eric
Bigger

**❝ I REMEMBER THE FIRST TIME MOVING TO LOS ANGELES AT THE AGE OF TWENTY-TWO.** I had nothing but $1,000, my faith, my drive, and a few contacts. I slept on someone's couch for one year and paid $500 per month with a minimum wage job and a college degree. I say that to say this: dreams come true because today I am traveling and doing the things that I love! It has been a difficult journey, but now the journey continues, this time with hope and promise. Therefore, the message is this: 'Never, ever give up! Keep FIGHTING!' I am honored to be teamed up with The NYLON Project supporting those in need."

## HOMELESS INDIVIDUAL

"I left my home in Texas at the age of nineteen to pursue my dream of becoming an entertainer and musician at a cabaret in Miami. I saw an ad on Craigslist, and after a very promising call, I had my parents sell their most precious belongings so that I could make the move. Upon arriving in Miami, I realized that it wasn't at all what I thought, and the pay was almost nonexistent. I had too much pride to call my parents and tell them it was a fraud. In the beginning, I was able to find a few jobs here and there so I could rent a bed and buy a sufficient amount of food to get by. Eventually, the jobs became obsolete, and I found myself too tired to keep going. Today, I am homeless in Miami Beach and perform when I can to see what can come of it."

@ERICBIGGER

Holly
*Glasser*

# MEMOIR/LIFE LESSON

"Our lives can often seem so perfect and charming to the outside viewer in a world of carefully curated images on social media. From a quick glance, I appear to be a world-traveling fashion editor, actress, model, and singer living a glamorous lifestyle with ease and privilege. What you don't know is that my apartment flooded in Los Angeles forcing me to move all of my belongings into storage when I launched my magazine. On top of burning through a large chunk of my savings that first year as I learned to manage an entire company on my own, I faced setback after setback with my family, boyfriend, health, and more. I finally moved back to my apartment only to hear a still, small voice from God, whispering, 'Move out again. Put your things back in storage, and get ready to go where I am sending you next.' God was pushing me to the next level in life. No longer did I want to live in an apartment in the safety of those four small walls. I wanted a large house, an office for my company to grow my business exponentially, to travel the world, and to give back to my community. Now I just needed the faith to propel me to make this big step in life! Before, in my cozy apartment, I had grown safe and had plateaued in life, not allowing myself enough space to grow professionally or personally as much as I had dreamed of.

By letting go of my security blanket and taking a leap of faith, I made room for amazing change!

Traveling from New York to Los Angeles and Europe out of two suitcases without a home to call my own, I lived like a real gypsy for a bit to connect with God's true purpose for my life. I subleased with friends wherever I went, sometimes last minute. Living in chaos forced me to take my dreams seriously. It pushed me out of my comfort zone and into the wild unknown. It was all or nothing! Learning to rely on the divine Creator in the midst of uncertainty taught me compassion for others who struggle day to day, it taught me faith for my future, and most importantly, it taught me to be brave and go after my highest dreams.

Perhaps life has you in a tough place. Perhaps you have been homeless or lost everything or had a major setback. Remember to look up and look all around at all the beauty there is to see, and I believe you will always find a helping hand. Take that hand, and one day, maybe you will be the hand that helps someone else stand up. Make your life count. If you're reading this, I know there is a reason for that. Keep up the good fight, and never give up on your dreams. God gave you those dreams for a reason. You have a divine purpose for being right where you are. You are exactly where you are supposed to be today. That can change tomorrow, and it will. Keep growing, keep reaching, and let the setbacks be lessons and scenic detours, not your final destination!"

@HOLLYGLASSER

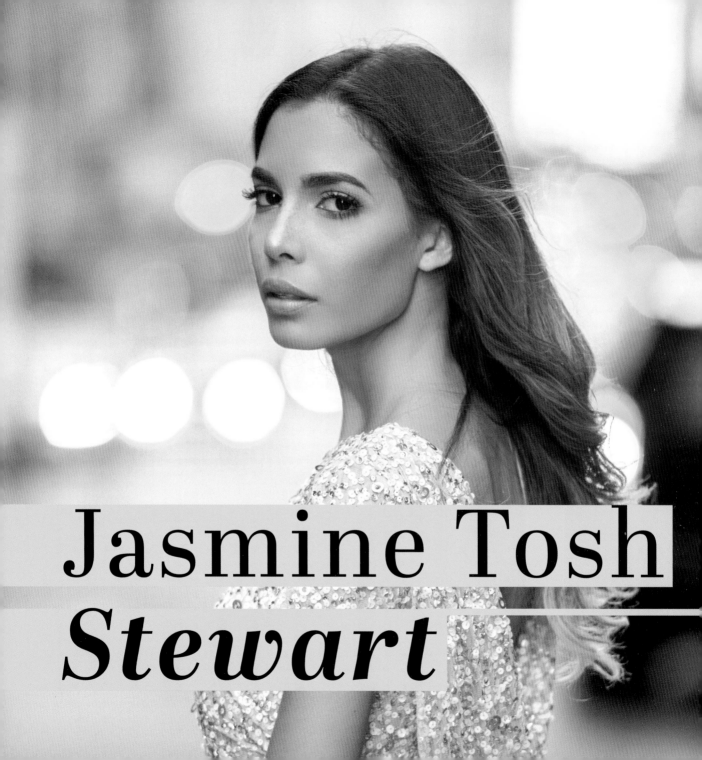

# Jasmine Tosh
## *Stewart*

# MEMOIR/LIFE LESSON

"I grew up in Los Angeles and went to various high schools in Northern Virginia. After I graduated high school in 2008, I did not want to go to college right away and decided to pursue my modeling career full time. I moved back to LA at the age of eighteen and lived there for one year, chasing my dreams. Although I loved it in LA, it was too expensive for me to live there. I had been working as a model and an actress (print jobs, commercials, and small jobs as a background actor), and it wasn't working out for me financially. I couldn't afford to do anything or even eat where I wanted to. When I turned twenty, I decided to move to Miami. I had never been there before and had no idea what to expect, but I was ready for change. I packed all of my things in my car with my rescue dog, Duchess, and drove down. I have always been adventurous, but I can't believe how much courage I had at just twenty years old to move to a new state all on my own. I wasn't afraid; it was almost like a calling from the universe.

I am twenty-seven now and am so happy to have made that decision when I was younger because my life has changed forever for the better. I have been living in Miami, Florida for almost eight years and love it here. When I arrived here in 2010, I continued my modeling career and began traveling to places I never had the opportunity to go to before, such as the Caribbean Islands. The geography is completely different in Florida; it was almost as though I moved to a different country. It was nothing like LA. I was so naïve that I didn't even know the difference between Miami and Miami Beach. I remember driving down Interstate 95 toward downtown to my temporary apartment, and as soon as I saw the buildings, I smiled and said to my dog, 'We made it!' After signing with a modeling agency, I continued to work as a model. In my spare time, I would try to make as many castings as possible. I had to work two jobs—one in retail and one as a hostess—just to pay my bills. I had always been into fashion, and going into the fashion industry had always been my passion.

Luckily for me, the growth of social media over the years, including Instagram, had inspired me to create a blogging platform, where I began to document my outfits in 2013. Around this time, bloggers had become extremely popular. I was determined to make it as a blogger. Never quit chasing your dreams! They will come true!"

@JASMINE_TOSH

Jessica
Ross

**" SEVERAL YEARS AGO, I WAS LAID OFF FROM MY JOB.** Because I was an independent contractor, I was ineligible for unemployment. In order to survive, I had to ask my family for money and utilize all of my credit cards. Worrying about money all of the time was incredibly stressful. It took me eight months to find a job that paid enough to afford my rent and bills. I have no idea how I would have lived or avoided homelessness if it wasn't for my family's help and having good credit. For this, I will always be grateful."

# HOMELESS INDIVIDUAL

"When the market crashed, I lost everything. My father and mother had both died when I was younger. I hadn't gotten married, so I was alone. My friends—let's call them acquaintances—would tell me they didn't loan money to friends because it always created conflict. My credit wasn't so great because I often delayed my payments on credit cards, bank loans, etc. There was nowhere to turn and no money to be found. At that time, having a job was a luxury because even those who had a job were doing everything to keep their positions. Eleven months later, all of my savings were spent, and I found myself on the street. It's tough being alone. But now that I am on the street, all of us living without a home support one another. It's more support than I ever had when I was living in a home."

@JESSICAROSSOFFICIAL

Joice
*Oliveira*

"**WHEN I WAS NINE YEARS OLD, I WAS IN A SERIOUS CAR ACCIDENT.** I was with my two younger sisters and my mother. She was driving when a car hit us and fled without giving us any help. My sisters and I were okay. My mother, who was thrown out of the car, received several injuries when the car rolled over her twice. She couldn't walk for quite a while. It was a very difficult time. Thank God, my mother is now okay. I am so grateful for being alive and that my family is safe. At that moment, I realized how fragile life is, how fragile we were, and that had it gone differently, we wouldn't be here today. GRATITUDE."

# HOMELESS INDIVIDUAL

"I ran away from home when I was seventeen. I had a best friend who also was unhappy with the way her parents treated her, and she decided to join me on what we thought would be an adventure. We decided to hitchhike across the country to get as far away as we could from our toxic lives. More than halfway along the way, I will never forget the moment when I closed my eyes to take a nap. Minutes later, I heard a loud crash, and my body felt as though it was floating. I opened my eyes and saw flashing lights and ambulances. I don't remember much else. A few hours later, I woke up in a hospital bed and again, didn't remember much. However, what I do remember is that my best friend, who was with me on the ride, was nowhere to be found. I got the gut-wrenching news that my best friend had not made it through the crash. I was now alone. I left the hospital, and since then, I have been living on the streets with no one. All I have is myself and my faith in God. Although I don't have a place to live today, I have my health, which I am thankful for every day."

@JOICEOLIVEIRA

Jordan
*Gill*

# RESILIENCE: THE STORY OF MY FATHER

"I have been fortunate enough to live a very blessed life. I have my health, family, friends, a good job, and a roof over my head. My dad, however, did not have the same charmed childhood. This is a story about him. Had he had not overcome all of his hurdles growing up, I would not be so fortunate today.

When my father was two years old, his house burned to the ground. His father escaped, but his mother didn't. His brother rescued him from his crib, saving his life. After the tragedy, his dad put him and his brother up for adoption as he was unable to support them.

Fortunately, he and my uncle were adopted by a nice family who already had three kids. Their family grew from five to seven. They had plenty of love to give, but not nearly enough resources. My dad grew up extremely poor in government housing in Flint, Michigan. He barely had enough to survive. Regardless, he was very determined to succeed. He was able to secure a grant from the State of Michigan to send him to college at Michigan State University. He hitched a ride to move to East Lansing and worked odd jobs while in school to pay to live. He graduated with an engineering degree and now is able to easily provide for his family. An overcomer, he learned the hard way the importance of resilience and the struggles it takes to succeed."

@NEWYORKCITYSTYLIST

Josh Heffler

# STORY OF PERSEVERANCE, WHEN FACED WITH CHANGE

"When I was twenty-four years old, I was forced to make a decision that would change my life forever. I grew up living and breathing business since my father, grandfather, and great-grandfather had spent their lives serving in the fast-paced financial industry. After our family dinner every night, I would spend two or more hours talking business and financial strategies with my father instead of playing video games like a normal sixteen-year-old. My father's influence and mentorship led me to desire a life in finance. The plan was that I would take over the family business someday. All of that changed when an offer was made to acquire the business—an offer that was hard to pass. My entire career path and life would change that day in the blink of an eye.

After the company sale, I was forced to decide between becoming a slave to a corporate company at a three percent raise for the rest of my life or start from scratch. I decided to leave the finance industry in pursuit of another sector I was passionate about, considering the exponential growth opportunity: entertainment.

I took all of my savings and started a company called LineRocket Entertainment. I risked the majority of my net worth building a new company and investing in various entertainment platforms, which could have ultimately bankrupted me and sent me down a negative path that would have been tough to recover from. After the ups and downs of a five-year struggle learning how to run my own company, LineRocket Entertainment finally grew into a successful concert and live event business that donated a portion of all proceeds to various charities.

I will always remember how my high risk turned into a high reward, and that confidence has led me to my most recent endeavor of sending Lady Gaga to outer space in a Virgin Galactic space shuttle for the first-ever live concert outside the Earth's atmosphere. Dreams do come true when you go outside of your comfort zone!"

@JOSHHEFFLER

Julia
*Faria*

# INSPIRATIONAL MEMOIR

"This life is truly very crazy. It's scary. It's simply a breath. You turn a corner and can be surprised. You can bump into the love of your life or trip and twist your ankle. We never know. All we know is that we are alive. At the age of seventeen, I was super alive, living my life intensely. I was working my first job. I'd go and come back by taking a ride with my father, since I still wasn't driving, and we practically worked in the same building. I spent almost two years of going to work in the passenger seat of my father's car. A year and a half later, I decided to go on a well-deserved, one-week vacation on the beach with a group of friends. When I returned, life took me by surprise. A lot had happened back home while I was swimming in the ocean. Instead of telling me what happened while I was away, my family waited until I returned.

On my first night out while on vacation, which was the first night that my father came back from work alone in the car, he was in for a surprise. Stopping at a light, he moved to change the song on the radio and was so focused on what he was doing that he had no idea what was happening when he heard a loud sound and saw that a robber had shattered the passenger window into pieces. The robber, who got spooked when he thought my father was moving to attack him, shot his gun. The bullet grazed my father's head, which only lightly burned him. While everything happened quickly, what scared my father the most was the realization that the bullet made a hole in the passenger seat and in the exact level of a person's chest.

The bullet went directly to the passenger seat of the car and made a hole. The hole was made where the chest of the person sitting there would've been, and I am not being dramatic. So much so that we kept the car for several years following, and the hole stayed there. The thing is, had I not gone on vacation, it would have been me who would've died. Because of one day—one, tiny day—everything could've been different. Crazy!

Today, my father celebrates my birthday on the day that this accident took place. And I, who had been already living my life intensely, live life even more. I give myself to whatever comes my way. I try to laugh more than I cry. I go after the life I want to live. As I started saying at the beginning of this story, life is simply a breath. And because of that, we can't allow any opportunities to pass us by."

@JULIAFARIA

Justin
Bullock

# FORMERLY HOMELESS & STILL FIGHTING

"My whole life, from birth until now, has been an everlasting struggle. I am struggling as I type this as I think about what's next in my life. What's the next move? The next place to call home? If I had to describe a particular time, it would be when our family was evicted from our home and everyone being separated after always having been together. How I overcame that and am still over-coming that on a daily basis, has been by being the best 'me' I can be. I have to never stop doing what I love—no matter what—in the hope that it will all be worth it one day."

@JERRBUL

Kasey
*Ma*

# WORDS OF WISDOM/INSPIRATION

"Have you ever worked so hard for so many years only to realize you can't get any better? That was the case for two of my passions: swimming and singing.

When I was twelve years old, I was accepted into the Junior Olympics for swimming; however, I could not attend. It was not because I was sick or could not afford the flight, but rather because my knees gave up on me a bit faster than I did. A couple of weeks prior, I had injured myself while running during dryland exercises. I was diagnosed with bilateral chondromalacia patella. In short, the cartilage that stabilized my knees had worn down so much that my tissues were beginning to erode. The doctor said I would either have to stop swimming rigorously or get knee surgery. I was devastated. I had been training to be an Olympic swimmer since the age of eight. Now my dreams were taken away from me. Having surgery wasn't an option because it would stunt my growth. I had no other choice but to stop swimming competitively. I went through intensive physical therapy to help bring me back to recovery, but it was never the same. My knee injury was permanent. I cried for many months. To this day, it is still hard to accept that I can't lead the active lifestyle that I desire.

I am a big believer in the saying that when one door closes, another opens. Fortunately, that other door was my passion for music. Although established as a piano player, I wanted to add another element of music into my life: singing. A year or so after discovering my knee problems, I fell in love with the art of singing and did not hesitate to explore my newfound interest. I was so excited when my first voice lesson took place. Unfortunately, as I began to sing, I realized I could not sing for more than fifteen minutes before my throat would start to hurt and my voice became hoarse. My teacher recommended that I visit the doctor. When I did, I discovered that I had built up scar tissue on my vocal folds that were preventing me from safely singing. The only option was to have surgery or stop singing. I couldn't believe it! After many years of getting over the fact that I had to abandon my love for swimming, I found myself with the same kind of physical predicament with singing. There was no way I was going to let my dreams get taken away from me again.

I decided to go through the surgery. I am happy to say that I could not have made a better decision. Recovery was brutal, but it was worth it. Fast forward to today, and ten years of voice lessons, I can say that the endurance of my voice is not only stronger, but also my singing has improved quite a bit.

Although my first failure with swimming was devastating, I am so thankful for the courage I had gained from going through it. I unearthed a new talent and other interests in the arts, such as fashion, and I was able to keep them all in my life. Through the many struggling years, I have learned to never, ever give up on something that makes you happy and makes you whole. There will be other opportunities, and you will stand up again!"

@THESTYLEWRIGHT

# Kelly of
# *Mimosas &*
# *Manhattan*

I did everything in my power to ensure my bosses and clients were happy. I continually found myself in situations where I was being sexually harassed by my clients, and even worse, my bosses were turning a blind eye to 'keep the good business.' For a long time, I didn't leave because I was embarrassed, naïve, and honestly thought that was just how the industry worked. Until one night, the situation got completely out of hand, and I couldn't take it anymore. I quit my job two weeks later without another job lined up or even a single interview scheduled because I knew I had to get myself out of the situation. I struggled financially for months, but removing myself from a toxic environment for the sake of my wellbeing was too important to continue to brush the problem under the rug."

# HOMELESS INDIVIDUAL

"I didn't know any different. When I was a little girl, I thought any physical connection with a man was affection and love. As I got older, I realized that there was a problem. The 'love' I thought I was getting was strange. Eventually, I learned that I was being sexually assaulted. I tried to tell my mother that her boyfriend was inappropriate with me. She continually told me that I was mistaken. I started to feel both crazy and ashamed. He wound up turning my mother against me since I didn't have the courage to speak up more and ask for help. Because of my fear, I was kicked out and had nowhere to go but the streets. The streets became my safe place. Today, it's where I live and where I call 'home.' Any place is better than where I thought was 'home.'"

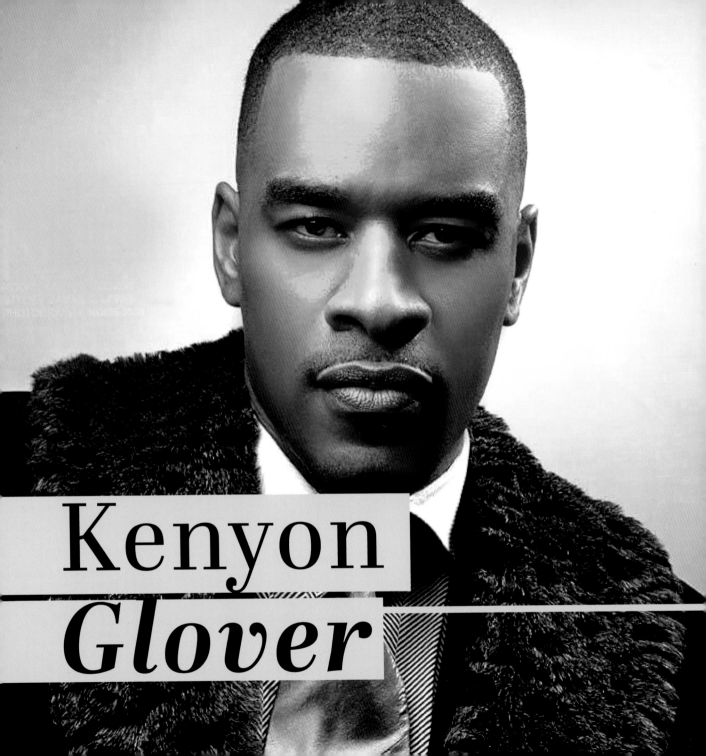

# Kenyon
## *Glover*

**"THE BIGGEST PERSONAL STRUGGLE I HAVE HAD TO FACE AND OVERCOME IS THE TIME** when my doctor told me that my NBA career was over due a knee injury. That was the most devastating thing that I have ever faced. At that very moment, all I could think about was committing suicide as soon as I left his office and got home. I did attempt suicide. Although I haven't overcome it completely, I have been able to sustain my sanity by surrounding myself with positive and uplifting people and by finding and doing other things that I love, which has motivated and encouraged others to chase their dreams and let absolutely NOTHING stop them!"

# AUTHOR'S NOTES

Mental illness is a significant cause of homelessness. Many of the homeless individuals we encountered, when faced with this type of challenge, wound up becoming mentally unstable. They end up living a "fake" life—one in which they aren't allowed to lead. Due to this, they stay stagnant, lose everything (since they are not making an income), and wind up on the streets.

@KENYONDGLOVER

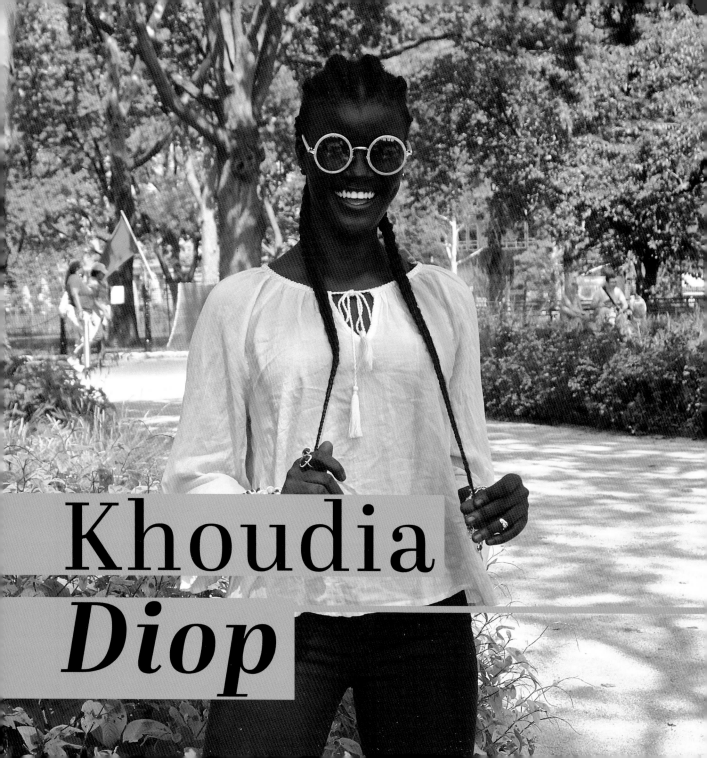

# Khoudia
# *Diop*

# WORDS OF LOVE/EMPOWERMENT

"I was picked on by other kids when I was younger because of the darkness of my skin tone. But this is something that is actually quite normal in Senegal, where I'm from. It's not a nice feeling, and I've had to learn to love myself more every day by tuning out the negativity, which helped a lot. They called me 'midnight,' 'mother of the stars,' 'darkness,' 'darky,' and 'too black.' It was horrible and mean. Eventually, I learned that these kids didn't love themselves, and that bullying came from their insecurities. When the bullying started, I would confront the bullies by standing up for myself. I eventually learned to be more confident and love myself. In time, I did not have anything to prove. I came to a point where I could tune out the negativity and not feed into it. Having support from family, friends, and now fans definitely helps affirm what I already know: that I am worthy, loved, and beautiful! I wish everyone could realize that and feel that way. Once I saw myself, I started to find things I liked about me. Then I learned to love myself and to celebrate my unique beauty. That also helped me to feel the same way about others. I could even feel positively about the people who bullied me because I knew they were just displacing their hurt on me. Today, I am able to spread the message of love in beauty to everyone."

@MELANIIN.GODDESS

# Lara
# *Eurdolian*

" GROWING UP, I LEARNED VERY QUICKLY THAT LIFE COULD CHANGE IN THE BLINK OF AN EYE. My parents separated when I was five years old, and we went from living in a big house with my own room and a pool, to a small apartment where I shared a room with my sister. While I'm now very grateful for everything I had and everything my mom sacrificed, it didn't always feel that way. I grew up in a very privileged town, which made me very self-conscious about our living situation. I went from being the kid who had big birthday parties and having my entire class over to feeling embarrassed when friends would ask to do sleepovers, or their parents would offer to give me a ride home. We also had to make compromises and choices based on our finances.

One year, just before Christmas, my cat, Moushi, got really sick, and we had to take him to emergency care. He was hanging on by a thread, and the doctor wasn't very optimistic. He suggested we put him down. My mother was desperate (she saw the looks on our faces) and asked the doctor if there was anything that could be done. Reluctantly, he gave us the option of putting Moushi on an IV overnight. When my mom found out about the cost, she said it was either Christmas presents or the treatment because we couldn't afford both. Even with the odds against our cat, we picked him without thinking twice. There was probably some type of life lesson I learned in that moment, especially since Moushi survived.

Over time things got better, thanks to my mom, who somehow championed a full-time corporate job while raising two demanding girls. We upgraded to larger apartments and our own rooms, and by the time we were teenagers, we were living in a house again. While life would have been much easier if we never had to worry about finances, I'm grateful for everything I learned during my childhood. From working hard to budgeting and prioritizing my paychecks, these were skills I learned early. And as soon as I was old enough to work, I did, from babysitting to working retail through high school, and then working my way through college. I've always had multiple jobs and felt the importance of planning for my future and having a nest egg. I've also never lived beyond my means or even spent my bonus checks. Extra income always went straight into the bank as if it never existed. For me, extra savings in my account always felt like extra security in life. Even though I've had a lot of success throughout my career, I've never lost the fear of losing it all, which has always helped motivate me to succeed and do better."

# HOMELESS INDIVIDUAL

"Poker. Blackjack. Craps. All of these games have consequences, and I learned them the hard way. We had a good life from what I remembered growing up as a kid. However, my father was a gambler. It started as fun and games, and then when the money started running out, his addiction got him to where he was gambling away our belongings, including our basic life necessities. We wound up losing everything. My mother became deeply depressed and eventually hung herself. My father left, and I don't know what happened to him. I did have the chance to recoup and win again in life and went to live with my aunt. However, drugs got the best of me. Drugs were the only thing I knew that could erase the memories (my mother, my father, the suicide, etc.). My aunt couldn't deal with my addiction. It was a lot more than what she had signed up for. I wound up on the streets, where I have people who understand."

@PRETTYCONNECTED

# Laurissa
## *Lala*

**" WHEN I WAS FOURTEEN, I WAS DIAGNOSED WITH CROHN'S DISEASE.** I lived in crippling pain almost all of the time for a year before I knew what was wrong. I ended up losing my mobility and had to relearn to walk. I was always very athletic, so this really took a toll on me. I also had a love for performing, especially singing. Because I lived in bed for so long, I used art and music as my therapy, which I believe healed me. Music has always been there when I needed it. It's been able to make me feel strong again, and I want to share that with the world."

# HOMELESS INDIVIDUAL

"The war was brutal. It crippled me. I came back and had a little (very little) help from the government. I needed more than what they offered to keep my health insurance, house, and bills aligned. I fell behind on payments. When I lost my house, I was shocked to see that I had fellow veterans on the streets—others like me. More support needs to be available for us after fighting for our country. It's time to take a stand. Maybe people like you can finally showcase our voice."

@INTHELANDOFLALA

Linh
Dao

# WORDS OF WISDOM/INSPIRATION

"Hi, my name is Linh Dao, and I currently live in Los Angeles, California. I was born in Vietnam, and I moved to the United States seventeen years ago. Growing up, my family wasn't exactly the wealthiest; however, we were not homeless. My family has always been hardworking people. It didn't matter what jobs we worked. We always made sure to put in one hundred percent commitment to be financially independent. I see it in my grandparents, aunts, uncles, my parents, and other relatives. They have always made it a goal to hustle, making sure to provide food for the family at the end of the day. Money was not something we took for granted, and even until today, money has never come easy. When we have it, we spend it wisely. I saw the struggle my family went through and still goes through to make sure we would never be homeless. I learned to appreciate life even more, and because of the hard work that my family put into their daily lives to make a living, I am now the person that I am. I've learned so many valuable lessons by watching my family work hard to make a living. They taught me never to quit, always be humble, not be afraid to ask for help, etc. The skills I was taught are very useful in life. My family and I overcame the financial struggles by working hard for what we want and never quitting when life got hard. Put in time and effort into what you do every day, and the results will come. We make the best of our situation and are thankful for what we have and cherish it."

@XCAPEWITHLINH

# Lorena
# *Branquinho*

# WORDS OF WISDOM/INSPIRATION

"The story I will share with you all today happened to me a long time ago. I never had the courage to tell anyone, except for a few people who were pertinent in my life at the time. I have worked since I was a teenager. Working always made me very happy. My parents taught me from an early age to value everything that we receive. They also taught me to work and fight for what we want, and because of these lessons, I began working at the age of fourteen. I didn't have a fixed income, but it was enough to help at home. I modeled; I worked events. Those were things that I truly enjoyed. I always loved having my independence without needing one hundred percent from my parents.

As the years went passing by, I met many people and had boyfriends. I went to college, and time started being more of a luxury with so many things to do. When I was twenty-three and had just returned from being an exchange student in California, I got into many discussions with an ex-boyfriend about not having enough time to go to parties, family birthdays, and even time for myself. I decided to let go of being a freelancer of many jobs and focus on just one job.

A friend of mine offered to share my resume at the job where she was working. She told me it was an amazing job. I accepted. I did the interview, and a month later, I was working full time. I was originally hired to be an administrative assistant. One day, when I was at the reception desk speaking with a colleague, one of the owners came by, started staring at me, and said something like, 'Wow! You are a cutie, aren't you?' I didn't trust him the moment I met him. I looked at him and said, 'I will excuse myself now,' and went back to my office. In the days following, I noticed this man would show up and sit right next to me every time I would go have lunch. I started getting notes at my desk directly from him, stating that I had to get to know what 'a real man' felt like and that I needed to stop dealing with little boys. At that moment, I felt like the worst person in the world for having given him the right to tell me these things.

I started feeling bad. I wasn't sleeping, I couldn't eat, and just the thought of going to work started to get me anxious and nervous. His notes started coming in more often, and each time, I would get more and more anxious. One Sunday at the end of the day, I started crying and couldn't stop. My mother got scared. I couldn't explain to her what was happening. All I told her was that I didn't want to return to work. She got very upset. On Monday, I told my work that I wasn't feeling well and wouldn't be coming in. I called to set up an appointment with a psychiatrist. I went, cried a lot, and tried to tell her the maximum I could of the story. She gave me some antidepressants to calm down. From there, I stayed for three months inside of my room (I locked myself in). I didn't want to see anyone, speak with anyone, eat, or do anything. I was afraid to go anywhere when there were more than three people, which was weird, considering I've always loved people.

It was a very difficult and hurtful time for me, as well as my family. I started therapy, and after lots of conversations and self-reflection, I felt the need to be amongst people again. I decided to go back to the event industry to work with people, as I've always done. Little by little, I got better and started getting near people again in closed spaces. Today, my biggest love is being in the middle of lots of people and helping in any way with inspirations in the lifestyle and fashion world. However, from this experience, I have never been able to go back and work at a company; I like to have the liberty to do and go as I wish."

@LORENABRANQUINHO

# Lynnette
## Joselly

**" IN 2010, I HAD JUST GRADUATED FROM FLORIDA INTERNATIONAL UNIVERSITY WITH A BACHELOR'S DEGREE IN BUSINESS ADMINISTRATION.** I was eager to get out into the real world and do adult things, like move out of my mom's house, make big career moves, and, of course, make some money. Unfortunately, there was a reality check; I had high expectations for a salary that apparently needed much more than a degree to land a job. To build a portfolio of experience in the marketing industry, I had to do a few internships that did not include any pay. Finally, a year later, I got hired to work as a graphic designer and social media marketing assistant for a high-profile celebrity-events company. I felt like life was going well. I had a dream job, decent pay, and was enjoying my early twenties. Then BAM! Out of nowhere, without any notice, the company I was working for went bankrupt and refused to pay out their employees. This was one of the lowest points in my life as my grandmother had just passed away, I was unemployed, my car broke down, credit card companies consistently denied me, and the list went on. With a small savings account and a supportive and understanding family, I was able to overcome this stressful time. This struggle has taught me many lessons in life that have made me a smarter businesswoman today."

# HOMELESS INDIVIDUAL

"Coming straight out of college, I thought I had the world at my fingertips. Sure, I owed over twenty thousand dollars in student loans, but in my mind, with a degree, any job was possible, and I'd pay it back in no time. I come from a family where my single father makes minimum wage and works two different jobs. I thought that I was the one who would get my family back on their feet. Little did I realize that without experience, I, too, would make minimum wage. Both my father and I are in-and-out of shelter systems at the moment. They give us jobs; however, the jobs we get at the shelter systems are $7.50 an hour and sometimes a bit higher. Living in NYC, this type of salary does not allow us to leave the shelter life and be independent. Maybe one day, with my degree and a year of experience, I will get us both out and into a home again."

@LYNNETTEJOSELLY

# Maddi Jane

# WORDS OF WISDOM/INSPIRATION

"During the summer of 2016, in my hometown of Wheaton, Illinois, I watched my friends go off to college. I stayed home, knowing that my journey in music that began when I was eleven years old on the Ellen DeGeneres Show was worth continuing and that college would only be counter-productive for me. I was on the verge of final negotiations with a major label. A picture in my head of what the next year would look like naturally began to form, and I thought that picture was dependable. In the next month or so, everything crumbled. Red flags were revealed about the players involved, and it was clear to me that signing was no longer in my best interest. My adventure-packed picture of the future shattered. I was left with my thoughts, my computer, a room in my parents' home in the suburbs, and a million questions. Looking back, I now realize that those few months with what felt like nothing equipped me with some of the most pivotal sentences I hold onto that re-centered my priorities and gave me an understanding of life I would never have had before. During what felt like a loss, I gained so much. Here are some of the lessons I learned.

Helping people helps you more than them. I held my dreams loosely with not much else to do and let them fall temporarily to the back burner. I dove into the only thing that felt like a good use of time. I talked to strangers because I could. I taught picking patterns on a three-stringed guitar to a fellow musician who happened to be homeless, sitting on a street corner in Chicago. I got involved in a community a few blocks from me of refugees from Nepal and spent my time dancing with them, playing soccer, and learning their language. Activities of this nature took the focus off of my woes and enabled me to realize that there are many more important things in life than the subjects that occupy most of my attention. How could I be down because my big label deal fell through when my friends didn't have money for lunch? How could I feel unseen because I didn't get as many likes as I'm used to when these people walk down the street every day with hundreds of cars turning a blind eye? While my friends at school looked at my situation with pity, I suddenly felt lavishly blessed and grossly and unfairly fortunate. I felt foolish for how I had pitied myself before.

Holding your dreams loosely and letting them go lowers the stakes and can make them come to fruition sooner. During this time, I also was able to write songs like I never had before. I moved into an effortless season of inspiration. With no one else hearing the songs, but for me, I felt as if I'd already won ten Grammys. Because the music was honest, it was the kind I've always wanted to make. I experimented with Garage Band and then moved to Logic. Flash forward a year. I am writing this short reflection from the passenger seat of my Ford Fusion on Route 66 in the middle of Arizona. I am moving to LA to transition into a season dedicated more exclusively to music. But I am not going into it the way I would have before. Life is really crazy—crazier than I thought—and we need to look out for each other in it. I'm going to do what I was created to do; any success is extra. The ability to create is blessing enough in itself. Everything else is extra."

@MADDIJANEMUSIC

# Madeline
## *Stuart*

# STORY OF HOPE, PERSEVERANCE , AND PERSISTENCE

Madeline Stuart is a twenty-one-year-old model from Brisbane, Australia, and most notably dubbed by the press as "the world's most famous supermodel with Down syndrome." This incredibly courageous, beautiful, and talented young woman has had astonishing success in the short time she has been modeling and has captured media attention internationally. With three simple words, "Mum, me model," Madeline changed not only her own life but the lives of so many people with big dreams who didn't fit the mold.

In late 2014 when Rosanne, Madeline's mum, took her to a fashion parade, where Madeline's passion was born. With a willful spirit and defined goal, Madeline continued on her fitness regime to address her weight, a struggle for most people with Down syndrome. Inspired and undoubtedly proud, Rosanne photo-documented her daughter's journey. "It will take a lot of work and dedication, but if you want to commit to this journey, I'm with you," Rosanne told Madeline.

After losing forty pounds, a massive amount for anyone, Rosanne posted Madeline's before-and-after shots online, not only to show the dramatic results, but also to encourage others. She knew Madeline's story would resonate with people around the world. She wasn't wrong. Almost overnight, the post went viral. Madeline's social media numbers grew, as the photo gained over 6.8 million views, and she began to hit global headlines with publications in Iceland, Germany, the US, Australia, Mexico, Cuba, and the UK picking up her story.

Modeling offers followed soon after from big fashion labels and non-profits, and it wasn't long before she received her first offer to grace the runway in New York. Since then, Madeline hasn't looked back.

Madeline has modeled in countless fashion shows, including New York Fashion Week, Runway Dubai, Caspian Fashion Week Russia, and Mercedes Benz Fashion Week China. She has been featured in prominent international publications, including *Vogue*, *New York Times*, *Forbes*, and *ELLE*. She has also endorsed products, including JBronze by Jennifer Hawkins, Weetbix, VP Wow, and Flat Tummy Tea.

It is important to Madeline to support those that support others. As such, she supports several charities and non-profits, including Multi-Cap Foundation, Endeavor Foundation Australia, Silver Linings Project, Vets Intl, The DisABILITY Museum, The Carol Galvin Foundation, Kulture City, FUB Sweden, Inside Outside Dance Ensemble, Buddy Walk NYC, The NYLON Project, and the Special Olympics of New York.

In 2015, Madeline was awarded the prestigious Model of the Year Award at Melange, an international fashion show in San Francisco, and nominated for Pride of Australia and Young Australian of the Year Award for 2015 and 2016 and named model of the year for 2016 by World Fashion Media. All of this while managing her Brisbane dance school, Inside, Outside Dance Ensemble, participating in Special Olympic Games, and launching her 21 Reasons Why by Madeline Stuart fashion label, a fashionably casual-chic RTW line. For the last eight months, her journey had also been captured by B-Reel Productions for a documentary, released in 2018. Not bad for someone only two years into building what has become an enviable career.

Madeline has a great sense of humor and a contagious smile. Not content with simply making a career, she continues a hectic touring schedule, spreading the important messages of diversity, inclusion, and acceptance. She exudes confidence, and her warm and friendly nature endears her to even the hardest of crowds. She shares her story with the hopes of inspiring, encouraging, and educating others, proudly changing society's perception of people with disabilities, one photo shoot at a time.

@MADELINESMODELLING

# Maria
# *Sivakova*

# FORMERLY HOMELESS

"Shortly after I first landed in New York to pursue modeling, I was homeless. I had no friends, no family, and no agencies that wanted to sign me due to my height. Once my meager savings ran out, I spent several months on an acquaintance's couch, sleeping in my clothes and living out of my suitcase. I didn't have much money for food, so I ate McDonald's when I wasn't starving myself to stay skinny. I made it through these obstacles due to a life lesson I learned while taking care of my mother after she was diagnosed with breast cancer. She shared with me all of her regrets about not having lived her life to the fullest, so I promised myself that I would rather die chasing my dreams than not to chase them at all. No matter how tired I got in New York or how much I wanted to quit, I never stopped working. I refused to give up, to live an average, ordinary life, filled with 'what ifs' and 'if onlys,' a life defined by what I hadn't tried vs. what I had.

I've come a long way since I was a frightened Russian girl walking through Times Square, feeling alone in a sea of people. I've managed to build a name for myself as The Little Model, turning my height—something that I had always hated about myself—into my defining feature and using it to create my brand on social media. I'm not yet where I want to be in my career, but I wake up every day with the same drive that got me this far: to live on my terms, no matter what it takes."

@THELITTLEMODEL

Matt
**Munson**

**" I TRY TO TALK TO PEOPLE WHO ARE HAVING DIF-
FICULTY IN ROMANTIC RELATIONSHIPS.** Heartbreak
can be so deflating that it prevents us from being the best ver-
sion of ourselves in so many aspects of our lives. It was my frus-
tration with love and the pursuit of happiness that landed me
on a dating show. My experience there has helped me realize
how important it is to 'carpe diem' when it comes to finding
love and surrounding myself with people who make me want
to be a better man."

# HOMELESS INDIVIDUAL

"Finding a good man is very difficult. I saw my grandmother, my mother, and my friends all left alone in the most difficult of times.
I've always believed in fate until fate brought me here. AOL (America Online) was a big thing when I was younger, and I would go
into all of the chat rooms to find the love of my life. One day, I met hereforyou27. Everything on paper looked and sounded great,
so I gave it a chance. He lived in NYC, and I lived in Atlanta. I made everything happen to get to him as he promised he'd take care
of me and lots of other empty promises. I had to get rid of everything I had in Atlanta for what I thought would be a life-changing
experience. Once I came to NYC, I found out that he wasn't who he said. Going to NYC did change my life but not for the better.
Things took a turn for the worse, and I am now homeless. Even though I'm still looking for my prince charming, I'm starting to
lose hope."

@MATT_MUNSON_

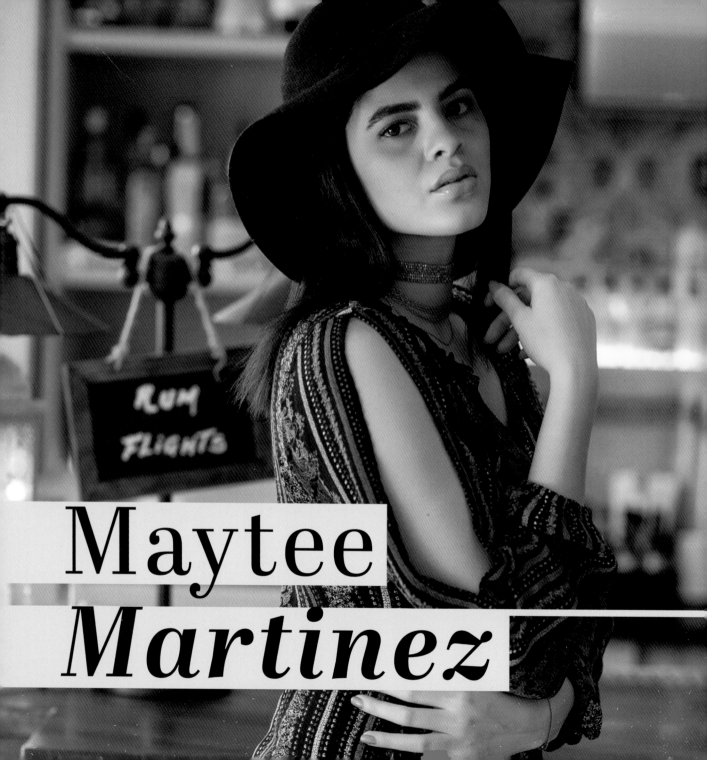

Maytee
Martinez

**66 THERE HAVE BEEN MANY STRUGGLES I'VE FACED IN MY LIFE.** I am grateful that God has always helped me in every situation. I remember, at one point, when my family and I had it all, and the next minute it was all gone. We had to start again from zero, but we never lost faith and hope. The lessons we went through are now blessings to us. Now, we are better than ever before, and thanks to the struggles, we are now stronger than ever."

# AUTHOR'S NOTES AND OBSERVATIONS

Throughout our research we had the pleasure of speaking to many homeless individuals, and we found that lots of them kept the faith and have a Bible. They all pray every day, waiting for help or a solution, and even though they are homeless and have lost everything, the things they never forget are their faith and hope.

@MAYTEEMARTINEZ

# Melissa
# *Molinaro*

# WORDS OF WISDOM

"When I first moved to LA, I went through a lot of financial struggles. I worked so many odd jobs just to make ends meet, but it still was never enough. I remember a time when I had no money even to buy toilet paper, so I would walk to Wendy's across the street from my place and would take stacks of napkins. LOL! I was a struggling actress in Hollywood and hustled any way that I could. I worked kids' parties, where I dressed up as Disney Princesses. I also danced at bar mitzvahs. I was a Skechers promotional model, handing out flyers on roller skates. I waited tables, was a Miller Light girl, a personal assistant—you name it! All I knew was that I was never giving up. I stayed persistent and focused on my goals. I started booking national commercials, guest-starring on TV shows and films, and releasing my music projects. I've had a lot of wins along the way, but never changed my work ethic. I'm still that girl, hustling in Hollywood. I've started my clothing line, MAE, and fitness brand, Move by Melissa, teaching my exclusive class, Power Booty all around the world. This is a very tough industry to be a part of. You really have to love what you do, be patient, and have faith that hard work and perseverance pays off."

# AUTHOR'S NOTES AND OBSERVATIONS

Many people living on the streets had the same beginning as Melissa, struggling to work many jobs to make it in the entertainment and fashion industry. However, not everyone makes it and end up using all of their savings trying. However, the spirit of wanting to be an entertainer remains, as they keep performing while living on the streets, in the hope that one day, they will be discovered and still have their big dream come to fruition.

@MELISSAMOLINARO

# Mitchell
# *Webb*

# WORDS OF WISDOM

"Prejudice: a word that is never too far from my mind. It's a word that is often associated with the underrepresented. Some may consider it cliché, but it's a very real concept for most LGBTQ+ community members and me. I have too often gotten up close and personal with it. It's something that, as a content creator with a predominantly straight-male target audience, I struggle with daily in my career. Growing up in the relatively small town of Essex, a suburban county on the outskirts of London, I knew I was different. There, everybody looks the same, dresses the same, acts the same, and mocks difference with an obnoxious label in the hopes to ultimately deter it. As I got older, I developed a deeper understanding and connection to fashion, art, and queer culture, but I knew most wouldn't understand that. I started to consciously change the way I acted and dressed to fit into the metaphorical 'tiny box' that was given to me, which infuriated me then and still does today. Why should I have to change the way I am to appease the small-minded? It's probably the oldest line in the book for my community and me, but one that still rings very true. It's often assumed that LGBTQ+ don't face prejudice in the fashion industry, but even now, in an established role, I find myself continually fighting against the tide.

I have no doubts that my social media following and blog audience would be larger, were I a straight man. As a men's fashion influencer, I make my living from providing inspiration, tips, and advice to men on their style. Unfortunately, most straight men in my experience have a chip on their shoulder about taking fashion tips from a gay guy. It's debilitating to my growth as a key player in this industry and something I personally struggle with every day. Even though I knew my family and friends would feel no differently once I 'came out' (a concept I find ridiculous), it was still the hardest thing I've ever done. I knew that society and daily life for me would change, as do all the other young people facing the same thing. Once you finally accept yourself and decide you are ready to open up to those you love, to be faced with rejection and prejudice is too often a point through which some don't make it. I did, but there are so many others who don't. According to the Albert Kennedy Trust, a quarter of the UK's homeless youth are LGBTQ+ young people who can't find their place in society because of simply being themselves. I'm still learning to accept that I am purely myself and nothing else. But the fact that something irrelevant to my expertise and profession, like whom I chose to love, directly affects my ability to establish myself more successfully, is an extremely hard pill to swallow."

# AUTHOR'S NOTES

It saddened us to meet individuals in the LGBTQ+ community on the streets because their parents and loved ones abandoned them. After the rejection of people closest to them, they also feel rejected by society.

Nadya
Rousseau

# FORMERLY HOMELESS

"I was eighteen years old when I moved to California to pursue my dream of being an actress. I didn't care that I had less than $600 saved from my part-time job at the YMCA or that my parents didn't entirely approve. I didn't care that I'd be living with my girlfriend's family, who had a history of being abusive. I also didn't care that I hadn't yet met with any Los Angeles modeling agencies and that this entire thing was a gamble. I just went for it. Living on nothing was scary but exhilarating. We accepted eating oatmeal and black beans every day; our weekly trips to the Pomona 99 Cent store were a pleasant ritual. Unfortunately, we couldn't find employment, and after three months, our frugal idyllic life folded. We became homeless when my girlfriend's brother stole the last couple of hundred dollars we had. We were homeless for two weeks and had no choice but to stay with the half-brother who robbed us. We slept in his van outside of motels in the San Bernardino area. One night, there was a carjacking right beside us, and we feared for our lives. It was the kindness of my girlfriend's sister and my parents that got us out of this situation. We ended up traveling cross-country from Los Angeles to Maryland on a train. After nine months of living in Maryland, working two and three jobs six days a week, we saved nearly $20,000 to move back to Los Angeles. This time, I had a modeling/acting contract in tow. That was 2006. I've now lived in LA for over ten years and have overcome other financial setbacks, including the Great Recession of 2008, at which point I thought I'd have to file bankruptcy. The key to success isn't money; it's resilience, gratitude, and ambition. Keep pushing forward, and always count your blessings, even when it seems like you have none left."

@NADYAROUSSEAU

Nic
Mora

**❝ I GREW UP IN AN AFFLUENT FAMILY.** My parents always made sure I had a job. There was always a roof over my head, and plenty of food to eat. I recently had to quit my stable job to be a full-time TV host and blogger. There were many times within the first six months when I didn't know how I would pay my next bill. Refusing to take any money from my parents, I went through most of my savings until, thankfully, I landed bigger deals. It was a very trying time for me with many moments of wanting to give up. Having a passion for ending homelessness since I was a kid. Even with my financial hardships, I contin-ued to feed the homeless around Los Angeles. Seeing people around my age in their twenties on the street sent a constant reminder that this could have easily been me. If my upbringing were different, if I had made one bad decision, if I had left my family, it could have easily been me. That memory will stay with me always."

# HOMELESS INDIVIDUAL

"I chose the streets because if I had stayed home, I would have had to live by my father's rules, which wasn't authentic to who I am or choose to be. I come from an affluent upbringing; however, if I want to have a few drinks on a daily basis and smoke some weed here and there, it's my choice to do so. Living on the streets is tough day-to-day, but it allows me to be who I want to be."

@NICMORAXO

Ray
Bentley

**"I STARTED TO DREAM BIG EARLY ON. IN MIDDLE SCHOOL, I WAS ALREADY TRYING MY HAND AT ACTING AND BEGINNING TO LOVE RAP MUSIC.** Growing up in a single income home left little money for pursuing these loves. At an early age, I learned that I had to work hard for these little extras in order to meet my goals. I delivered newspapers door-to-door for pennies. I saved up to make trips into Manhattan to land jobs as an extra on shows like Law and Order and Blue Bloods. During this time, I began writing my own song lyrics. Any free time away from school was spent on developing the start of my rap career. By the time I graduated from high school, I was ready to hit the recording studio. Again, money was a problem. But I found a way into the recording studio. I began taking on any part-time work I could find, this time while entering college and amassing more debt from student loans. During the summer months of my freshman year, I worked at a golf course, where my income came mostly from tips. At night, I ran a photo booth working weddings, graduations, and other events. Finally, I managed to save just enough to begin bringing my hard work into the studio. This led to performing live at local clubs and open-mike nights. After winning an open-mike night, which earned me a spot opening for Rich the Kid, I started to believe my dream just might be real. I'm currently looking to drop my first single, 'Buzzer,' soon."

## HOMELESS INDIVIDUAL

"I sing because it makes me happy. I perform because it's what I was born to do. Everything happens for a reason. I believe the reason why I ended up living on the streets was God's eventual plan for me to perform on the biggest stage in the world: New York City. Every day I have thousands in the audience, and my music reaches millions every year. I was born into homelessness, and I believe it was my destiny."

@RAYBENTLEYNJ

Sheree

# WORDS OF WISDOM AND INSPIRATION

"When I read people's stories about how they overcame hardship and struggles, it puts me to shame to compare. Quite frankly, I haven't had much REAL struggle in my life. Although I was born in China, I was fortunate to have a happy, healthy, and affluent childhood. My family owned a private architectural firm, quite a rarity in China back in the '80s when everything was owned and run by the government. We were the first to own many western technologies in our apartment building. I was flying around China at a young age with my parents as they went on business trips. That was thirty years ago, and China had yet to experience its technological and economic boom, so everything, even owning a piano at home as I did, was a BIG deal.

When I was eleven, my family emigrated to the US, hoping for a better life and education for me. My parents gave up their plummy lifestyle and came with just a few thousand dollars, as we left most of our familiar life in China. I remember them struggling during that time, trying to adjust to the sub-par lifestyle and downgraded societal status quo in the states while still trying to provide the best life they could give to me. My mom ran a daycare in our townhouse while my dad worked unfamiliar jobs as his previous studies and licenses didn't translate into hirable jobs. I got into a private college, and tuition was very expensive for out-of-state residents. My parents went above and beyond, trying to come up with the money to pay for it. That was the moment when I realized that I had to step it up and help. I was eighteen and shouldn't have been relying solely on my parents for financial support.

I told my parents that I would find ways to pay for my tuition, and I did. I took out a student loan and found a full-time job as a customer service rep at an internet start-up, plus various part-time jobs in the evening while attending school full time. I've done everything from waiting tables to singing at a karaoke bar, working for tips. It took me five years to complete all of my courses, but I was debt-free when I graduated. I paid everything off with my own dime and graduated with honors. It wasn't easy running on little sleep every day and studying for exams during my lunch breaks, but I never considered these things to be struggles or hardships, but rather life's experiences that shaped me to be who I am today.

I am so grateful for my parents and their selflessness and enormous sacrifices to give me a better future. Today, I am a mom of two. I will not hesitate to give up everything if it means a better tomorrow for them. However, I will want them to earn it, work for it, know the value of every dollar earned, and not take things for granted instead of feeling entitled. Life is very unexpecting; things can change suddenly, and I want my kids to develop life skills and social skills to help guide them when hardship occurs."

@BYSHEREE

Sierra
*Lorenzini*

**"I WAS A SMALL-TOWN GIRL FROM NEBRASKA WHEN I DECIDED TO MOVE TO NEW YORK CITY AT THE AGE OF EIGHTEEN.** I had high hopes and big dreams for myself, but it has been a story full of triumphs and struggles since not everything went to plan. I remember once looking at my bank account and seeing $200. It was a moment of reality that hit hard, and without family, I don't think I would have been able to make it. I am so fortunate for the support and love they have always shown me.

This past July marked ten years in New York, and as they say, if you can make it in New York, you can make it anywhere. I have built a life for myself that I am proud of, learning to stand on my own two feet and have surrounded myself with those who build each other up rather than tear each other down. From professional NBA dancer and captain to DJ to fitness model, nutritionist, Pilates instructor, and now blogger of Lorenzini Lifestyle, I can now say that moving to New York City was the best decision I ever made. I even found the love of my life in the midst of it all. And that, of course, is the favorite part of my story to tell."

# AUTHOR'S NOTES

As we shared in previous pages of this book, homelessness happens to many people who leave their small cities and come to New York City, Miami, or Los Angeles to achieve the BIG dream. Unfortunately, hurdles and competition get in the way, money runs out, and people are nowhere near their end goals. Many gifted people we spoke with on the streets don't have loved ones to help them out. So when you walk down the streets in these cities and it feels as though you are in a big concert, keep in mind that you are listening and seeing very talented people who went after their dreams at the wrong time. They are now trying to get heard or seen by someone who can change their destiny.

@LORENZINILIFESTYLE

Tezza

# BEAUTIFUL STORY OF TRIUMPH

"Almost seven years ago, I lost my younger sister, Sophie Rose Barton. We were two years apart, attached at the hip, and opposites in every way. Everything we did was together. Everything we planned, we planned together. When she passed away, all of my life plans crumbled before me in an instant. My sister and I played in a band for the last few years, writing songs, and playing gigs together all over the west coast. She was my rock and my center. I didn't know if I would be able to move on and continue to follow my dreams, our dreams. I had one of two options: to quit or to push on and fight all my pain or to feel the fear and do it anyway. After she passed, I decided to move forward and play music in honor of her. I have been so fortunate to carry on her legacy and to continue to change lives with music. My family and I have now started a music therapy foundation named after my sister, Sophie's Place. Sophie's Place, which is spreading through hospitals across the country, has not only become a beautiful representation of her but also touched the lives of many people. She lives on through her music. Moving through life with a purpose and for something bigger than yourself is like a sponge for opportunity. It opens doors to so many things and people, and I have since learned to be grateful for my trials."

"ENDURANCE IS NOT JUST THE ABILITY TO BEAR A HARD THING, BUT TO TURN IT INTO GLORY."
—William Barclay

@TEZZA

# Thania Peck

**❝ MY FAMILY AND I FACED A TON OF OBSTACLES WHEN WE IMMIGRATED FROM SOUTH AFRICA.** We lived in a poor neighborhood surrounded by gangs. Since we had a different accent and looked different, my siblings and I got bullied. The circumstances we were in didn't define me as an individual. I knew this wasn't the life I wanted to live. My parents created their own company, and as the business starting to grow, we moved to a better neighborhood.

Today, I live in Williamsburg in Brooklyn, New York. I work as a fashion lifestyle blogger with the company I've created, Catcher in the Style, Inc. Life has taught me lessons, but because I've been open to the universe, I always show gratitude. I know the sky is the limit to what you can do if you work hard and don't give up. I work with youth charities now because I think education for young people is essential. Perspective on life and confidence is everything. No one is going to create the life you want to live. You've got to create it yourself and not rely on others to make things happen."

# HOMELESS INDIVIDUAL

"Immigrating from Cuba when we did gave us a lot more hope. However, we left everything behind for refuge in the land of opportunity, the United States of America. Getting here was difficult, but once we arrived, day-to-day living proved to be more difficult than expected. Not speaking the language also made it hard for us to make strides in providing a life for our family. We have been going through the shelter system and have had help in improving our English. We hope soon to have a place to call 'home.'"

@CATCHERINTHESTYLE

# Thatyna Dhanyta *Braga*

# MEMOIR AND WORDS OF INSPIRATION

"My name is Thatyna Dhanyta Braga, and I'm from a town called Porto Alegre in Brazil. When I was seven months old, my parents and I were in a bus accident in which I suffered from head trauma and seizures. Because of this, the doctors said I wouldn't have a normal childhood. I could no longer play ball or participate in activities in which 'normal' kids participated. One of the effects of head trauma and seizures is that there's a good chance of experiencing difficulty when learning and even remembering random things. To the doctor's surprise, I learned to read before starting school at the age of five. This was a miracle. I started a course called 'Computer Kids' that teaches kids how to use a computer. As the years passed, I got into swimming, ballet, and piano. I also studied English as well as Spanish. However, due to all of these activities, I didn't have time to play with my friends.

When I was seven years old, my grandmother died due a mistake made at the hospital. It was terrible, and to be honest, it hurts to this day. From that moment, I started experiencing insomnia and developed bipolar symptoms. I started taking prescription meds. I began to see life a lot differently, and it was no longer the fairytale with a happy ending which I dreamed. I became a very sad child.

More years passed, and when I was finishing elementary school, another terrible thing took place. In the city in which I lived, it rained a lot, and for this reason there were always many floods. However, one, in particular, made us lose everything (we almost lost our lives.) My father decided to move us to the interior of Sao Paulo, where his relatives lived. That wound up being a bad decision as I wasn't happy and fell into a depression. I became anorexic and tried to commit suicide. I'd go to bed every night praying that I wouldn't wake up. The truth was that I didn't want to end my life; I just wanted the pain inside of me to go away.

Between the ages of twelve and fourteen, I remember being a huge fan of One Direction, Miley Cyrus, and Justin Bieber. Somehow my dream of meeting them one day kept me alive. I still remember the day that it was announced that One Direction would be coming to Brazil. A few days before the concert, I went through a make-over. I died my hair pink and this made me feel confident and happy. The concert was one of my best memories. My life changed two months later when I had a chemical reaction to the dye and lost all of my hair. I suffered bullying in silence because of that. As a result, my depression returned. I felt awful. I felt that I was never going to be pretty or good enough, which was killing me inside. I wanted to either die, live in a better world, or just sleep for years. My hair was everything to me, and so when I lost all of it, I lost myself, too.

In September of that same year, I was diagnosed with ovarian cancer on my right ovary. In November, a few days after my birthday, I had to have an emergency surgery to get it removed. After the surgery, I continued suffering from bullying for over a year, and I attempted suicide once again with a cutting knife. I still have the scar. After a short time, I decided to write my feelings down and because of this I received online help from people all around the world. Today, I help those who went through or are going through the same thing I did.

Currently, I am a digital influencer, writer, and activist. I enjoy studying psychology. I also take care of homeless animals. I still get treated for cancer with prescription medicine so I can have kids in the future. Fortunately, none of this keeps me from being happy."

@THATYNADHANYTA

# Valeria
## *Amaral*

# MEMOIR AND OVERCOMING STRUGGLE

"I was in my teenage years when Florida suffered from the real estate market crash. Other fraudulent activities also took place. My family was one of the many that fell victim to this. We were scammed into refinancing our home, and in turn, got evicted. This was devastating to our family. My mother went from having ownership rights to the home to no longer being allowed to live in 'our' home. I remember the day as if it was yesterday. It was Good Friday; we were put on the streets along with our belongings. We called our entire family, both my mother's and my father's side. My parents were divorced at the time. It was beautiful to see both families come together to help us to get our stuff off the streets and placed into storage and a roof over our heads. We were ashamed because of what had happened. We didn't want anyone to know. Due to love and support of family, we overcame it and got back on our feet. If it weren't for this, we would have been homeless. Being a part of this book means so much to me because if we didn't have people who love us, it would be a completely different situation. Everyone deserves this type of support, and it's very important to be grateful for everything you have. Always!"

# AUTHOR'S NOTES

Many people we spoke to lost everything with the real estate market crash and fraudulent activities, which took place in Miami.

@CHICBYV

Yessenia

**THE WORST MOMENT IN MY LIFE WAS WHEN I DEPENDED ON MY JOB TO GIVE MY FAMILY AND ME A GREAT LIFESTYLE.** I was ready to purchase a house, and I was so happy. But like they say, if you make plans, God has His own for you. Since I was laid off, I could not carry on with my house contract. I thought that I would immediately get a new job. Sadly, that was not the case. I was left living at my mother-in-law's house with a new baby on the way. I was completely shocked and felt so lost. I became depressed and lonesome. Even though I had my four-year-old and my amazing partner, I still felt like a failure. I searched for a job as if it was an addiction. I felt as if I was not secure enough. I think that when you have a beautiful family but are so riveted on your failure, you truly forget what's important. I immediately had a conversation with my parents, and they guided me to envision the light. I felt that I was blind for two years. Even though I appeared as a happy mom and a loving partner, my depression was winning. I was not happy, and everything seemed out of reach.

I finally managed to pick my head up high and focus on what truly mattered. I mattered. What I could offer mattered. I slowly started to love myself again and put my faith in God, trusting that I would overcome my season of darkness. Seven days later, I received a phone call for a job interview. Finally, I felt at peace with myself and began to live in the here and now. I learned to value and love what I had not obtained in those two years. I will never let depression win again in my household."

## AUTHOR'S NOTES

Many depressed homeless people today wind up giving up, feeling hopeless, and ending up losing everything because they lack the support of others.

@BEAUTYBEYONDFASHION

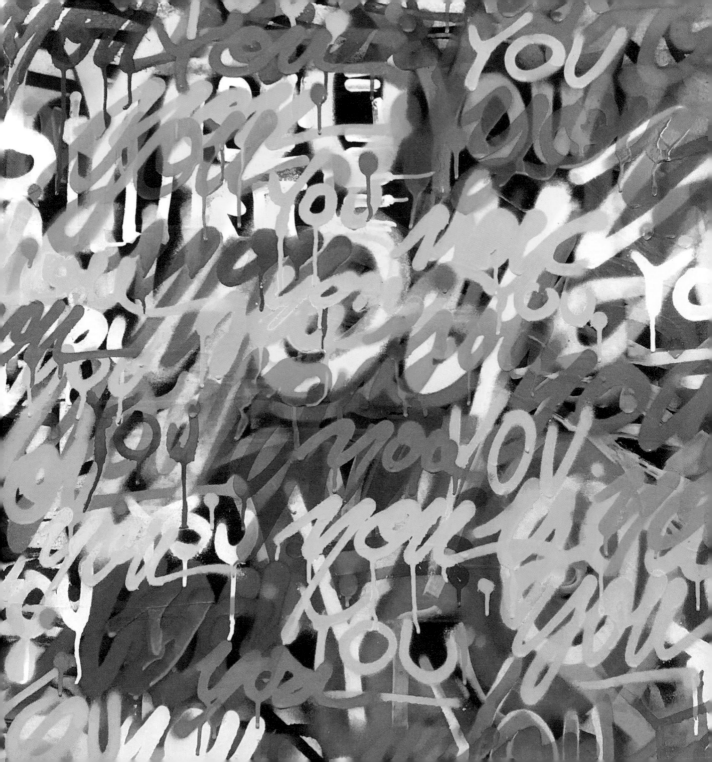